IMAGES
of Aviation

South Dakota Air National Guard's 114th Fighter Wing

On the Cover: Pictured are four 175th Tactical Fighter Squadron A-7Ds in a line formation flying above and to the south of Mount Rushmore Memorial, taken from an adjacent A-7D. (Courtesy 114th Fighter Wing.)

IMAGES
of Aviation

SOUTH DAKOTA AIR NATIONAL GUARD'S 114TH FIGHTER WING

Lt. Col. George A. Larson, USAF (Ret.)

ISBN 978-1-4671-0729-7

Published by Arcadia Publishing
Charleston, South Carolina

Printed in the United States of America

Library of Congress Control Number: 2021936759

For all general information, please contact Arcadia Publishing:
Telephone 843-853-2070
Fax 843-853-0044
E-mail sales@arcadiapublishing.com
For customer service and orders:
Toll-Free 1-888-313-2665

Visit us on the Internet at www.arcadiapublishing.com

This book is dedicated to the men and women who served at Sioux Falls Army Air Force base during World War II and with the 114th Fighter Wing, 175th Fighter Squadron, South Dakota Air National Guard.

Contents

Acknowledgments

I want to start thanking the governor of South Dakota (serving 2018–2022), also the commander of the South Dakota National Guard, the Honorable Kristi Noem, for her assistance in beginning the approval process on this book on the 114th Fighter Wing. I was granted approval for research on a US Air Force installation through the Air Force Book Program in New York City, New York. This allowed me to do research on the Air Guard installation. I researched photographs at Headquarters, South Dakota National Guard, Camp Rapid, Rapid City, South Dakota. The National Guard historian Durward Doering provided photographs and historical information on their Air National Guard wing. Due to COVID-19 restrictions, from April 2020 until January 2021, my research had to be conducted by internet. I want to thank Capt. Jessica Bak, who began my research. I then was assigned C.M.Sgt. Blake R. Parke, who became an invaluable research partner. He worked tirelessly to provide photographs on the history of the 114th Fighter Wing from its predecessor in 1942 to the present. I also received assistance on early historical photographs from Shelly Sjovoid, curator of the Siouxland Heritage Museums. Without these contacts' assistance, this book would not have been possible.

Introduction

The history of the 175th Fighter Squadron (FS) began with the World War II activation of the 387th FS, one of the original squadrons assigned to the 365th Fighter Group (FG) based at Richmond, Virginia, on May 15, 1942. The squadron trained to fly and maintain Republic P-47 Thunderbolts. The squadron's early combat missions were flown in support of the Eighth Air Force's Boeing B-17 Flying Fortresses and Consolidated B-24 Liberators flying high-altitude, daylight bombing raids to destroy German war production, transportation networks, supply depots, and oil production and refining to enable the Allied airborne and amphibious landings on D-Day (June 4, 1944), as well as shooting down Luftwaffe aircraft.

At this time in World War II, the Sioux Falls, South Dakota, commercial airport became an important military installation to fight the war. It was later renamed Joe Foss Field (also known as Sioux Falls Regional Airport) in honor of Brig. Gen. Joseph J. Foss, a US Marine Corps World War II ace who fought Japanese fighters and bombers over Guadalcanal in deadly air-to-air combat. He shot down 26 Japanese aircraft in the grim struggle to secure Guadalcanal Island from the Japanese. After World War II, Joe Foss helped create the South Dakota Air National Guard. In 2020, the South Dakota Air National Guard's facilities looked like a small Air Force base but without base family housing units, commissary, or hospital.

The US Army Corps of Engineers developed the current three-runway configuration from 1942 to 1947. After World War II, control of the airport was returned to the City of Sioux Falls, with the south portion leased to the newly formed South Dakota Air National Guard, 114th FG.

During World War II, US Army Air Force Technical Training Command operated the airfield from July 6, 1942, to May 11, 1945, training radio operators and mechanics. More than 45,000 military personnel trained on the airfield, which at full capacity housed 27,954 Army personnel (officers, enlisted, trainees, and instructional staff). The school's trainees learned electrical and radio fundamentals, including taking a radio bearing and direction finding, Morse code, Super Heterodyne receivers, and other related equipment. The school had a total of 161 classes, each with 425–450 students to meet the war demands for this personnel.

On May 24, 1946, the US Army Air Forces, in response to drastic postwar budget cuts imposed by the Democrats and Pres. Harry Truman, the inactivated active-duty World War II Army Air Force unit designations were transferred to state National Guard units for the creation of a National Air National Guard organization. The World War II 387th FS became the 175th FS on May 24, 1946. But this was not to be an easy transition.

The 175th FS was assigned to the 132nd Fighter Wing (FW) at Des Moines, Iowa, Airport. The wing was equipped with the North American F-51D Mustang day fighter, along with several types of World War II–era support aircraft. September 18, 1947, is considered the date for the South Dakota Air National Guard's creation, concurrent with that of the US Air Force as an independent service along with the Army and Navy, due to the implementation of the National Security Act (1947). The 175th FS was organized and extended federal recognition on September

20, 1947. Its creation was led by World War II Medal of Honor recipient Joe Foss. On March 2, 1951, the 175th FS was federalized and brought to active duty status assigned to the 133rd FG to support the Air Force's commitment to the Korean War (1950–1953). It was redesignated as the 175th Fighter Interceptor Squadron (FIS), Air Defense Command (ADC).

In August 1951, the 175th FIS was assigned to Rapid City Air Force Base, east of Rapid City. Its mission was air defense, to protect the Convair B-36 (nicknamed "the Peacemaker") intercontinental nuclear strategic bomber, 28th Bombardment Wing, Strategic Air Combat. Shortly thereafter, in a major reorganization, the Air Defense Command responded to its difficulty operating under the existing wing base organizational structure, replacing its groups and wings with regional organizations. The 133rd Fighter Interceptor Group (FIG) was activated, and the 175th FIS was assigned to the 31st Air Division on February 6, 1952. It was released from active duty on December 1, 1952, with its mission, personnel, aircraft, and equipment assigned to the new 54th FIS.

Control of the 175th FIS was returned to the State of South Dakota on December 1, 1952, activated at Sioux Falls the same day, to be equipped with the World War II surplus F-51Ds, as before. In September 1953, the squadron was ordered to place two of its F-51Ds on the ground and ready-launch alert for 14 hours each day during daylight hours. The F-51D was not an all-weather day-night interceptor. The Air Guard was using World War II aircraft considered to be a stop-gap until the Air Force re-equipped its active-duty squadrons with turbojet aircraft, and as it modernized the force, the excess turbojet aircraft were released to the Air Guard. It took time to reach a favorable aircraft upgrade program.

On April 16, 1956, the 175th FIS was reorganized along the model used by the Air Defense Command, redesignating it the 114th FIG. Its core operational units consisted of the 114th Maintenance Squadron, 114th Air Base Squadron, and 114th US Air Force Dispensary. During the 1950s and 1960s, the 114th FIG was equipped with the Lockheed F-94 Starfire (1954–1958), Northrop F-89 Scorpion (1954–1958), and Convair F-102 Delta Dagger (1960–1970).

Because of US intelligence agencies' assessments in the 1970s, which re-evaluated the capabilities of the Soviet Union's military threat from massed strategic bombers to nuclear-armed intercontinental ballistic missiles, the Air Defense Command began reducing its fighter-interceptor strength under the reality that the Soviet Union was not going to build up its strategic bomber force to attack the continental United States. The 175th FIS was redesignated the 175th Tactical Fighter Squadron (TFS) on May 23, 1970, when the gaining command became the Tactical Air Command. The 175th TFS traded its supersonic F-102As for the subsonic North American F-100D Super Sabres (1970–1977). The next aircraft upgrade was to the Vought A-7D Corsair II (1977–1991). The last F-100D departed Joe Foss Airfield in June 1977. In 1979, the squadron began 12-year participation in Operation Coronet Cave at Howard Air Force Base, Panama, protecting the Panama Canal, especially the vulnerable locks, from possible air attack. Squadron aircraft, aircrews, and support personnel first deployed to Howard Air Base in the summer of 1979 during the Nicaraguan Crisis. The 175th TFS was awarded the Armed Forces Expeditionary Streamer for its participation in Operation Just Cause to replace Panama's ruler Manuel Noriega, which allowed the nation's transition to a democratic government.

Tactical Air Command began retiring its A-7Ds in the late 1980s, with the Air National Guard transiting to the General Dynamics F-16C Fighting Falcons, a multirole supersonic fighter. The first three F-16Cs landed at Joe Foss Field, 114th Tactical Fighter Group (TFG), on August 14, 1991 (1991–present). In June 1993, the 175th TFS deployed eight F-16Cs to Brustem Air Base, Belgium, to participate in Operation Coronet Dart to support the European Exercise Central Enterprise. In December 1993, the squadron, for the first time in a combat deployment, deployed to Incirlik, Turkey. Its mission was to patrol the air space over northern Iraq, enforcing the no-fly zone and protecting Kurdish refugees in the area. The squadron flew these patrols from December 1993 to January 1994.

The 114th TFG was redesignated the 114th FW in October 1995 after the South Dakota Air National Guard adopted the "objective wing" organization used by the Air Force. The 175th FS was assigned to the 114th Operations Group, which subsequently was tasked to support Operation

Northern Watch from Turkey in 1995 and Operation Southern Watch from air bases in Kuwait in 1998 and Saudi Arabia in 2001.

The history of the Air National Guard took on a completely unexpected mission after the terrorist attacks on the United States (the first since the Japanese attack on Pearl Harbor, Hawaii, on December 7, 1941) on September 11, 2001. Hijacked commercial turbojet passenger liners flown by Muslim terrorists (who were able to take flying lessons in the United States undetected by US intelligence agencies) were deliberating crashed into highly visible targets.

In addition to the 114th FW's ongoing tasking as part of the US Air Expeditionary Force, unit members were activated to support Operation Noble Eagle, where reservists provided security within the United States, and Operation Enduring Freedom (America's global war on terrorism). Other deployments were to Balad Air Base, Iraq (October–December 2006, June–September 2008, and January–April 2010).

The 2005 Base Realignment and Closure Committee recommended that the 175th TFS retire its Block 30 F-16Cs and upgrade to Block 40 F-16Cs, which would give the South Dakota Air National Guard more operational capabilities. The first Block 30s entered the active Air Force inventory in 1982. Even though the Air National Guard constantly upgraded its Block 30 F-16Cs, the Block 40 F-16Cs provided deployment of enhanced guided weapons for improved ground attack, with longer launch ranges and accuracy. The first Block 30 F-16C was flown to the 309th Aerospace Maintenance and Regeneration Group, Davis-Monthan Air Force Base, Arizona, on May 7, 2010. The unit slowly swapped out the Block 30 F-16Cs for Block 40 F-16Cs.

The 114th FW won the Golden Eagle Award, presented during the Air National Guard Retention and Annual Training Conference held at Gulfport, Mississippi, in March 2019. The award recognizes the top state recruiting and retention team in the National Guard. The 114th FW achieved 106.3 percent overall personnel strength, the highest of 90 National Guard wings in the United States. This was the first time the 114th FW received this award at the national level. The wing was also awarded top honors at the regional level, winning the Golden Award for the top state as well as the Patriot Team Award for the top wing in Region II.

US senator John Thune (Republican, South Dakota) likes Sioux Falls' chances to upgrade the 114th FW with the new Lockheed Martin F-35 Lightning IIs in the coming years. The South Dakota Air National Guard, 114th FW, is positioning itself to be among 18 locations in consideration to base the F-35A Joint Strike Fighter. Without its record of excellence at the base documented by numerous awards, Senator Thune indicates that the wing would not even be considered as one of two guard units that will end up housing the new fighter jets.

Senator Thune has indicated that a committee of US Air Force officials that will make the selection will use an objective and "formulaic process" of reviewing metrics like overland airspace to allow for training exercises, runway capacity, and general infrastructure. The City of Sioux Falls will also play an important role in the review process. The standing of the base in the community will be considered by the selection committee, something that could also aid the 114th FW's ability to bring the US military's most advanced fighter to its Air National Guard base.

To ensure that the community is on board, South Dakota Air National Guard officials are working with Senators Thune and Mike Rounds, along with US representative Dusty Johnson and a military task force with the Sioux Falls Area Chamber of Commerce, to send a clear message to Pentagon officials that Sioux Falls wants and welcomes the F-35As. The mayor of Sioux Falls and other city officials met with 114th FW leaders, and a resolution of support from the Sioux Falls City Council was passed. The 114th FW and the South Dakota Air National Guard at Joe Foss Field is a viable option for stationing the F-35As, replacing the F-16Cs. If chosen, the 114th FW could add 45 employees to its 1,030 Air Guard personnel. This will be a manning increase in dollars into the local economy as Ellsworth Air Force Base, to the west of Rapid City, is expected to begin the transition from the B-1B Lancer bomber to the next-generation B-21 Raider bomber.

The initial Air National Guard unit employing operational Lockheed Martin F-35A Lighting II fighters was the 419th FW at Hill Air Force Base, Utah. The second was the 158th FW at Burlington Air National Guard Base, Burlington, Vermont. More Air National Guard units are scheduled to be equipped with F-35As in 2023: Truax Field Air National Guard Base, Madison, Wisconsin; and Dannelly Field, Montgomery, Alabama. As F-35A production increases, Air Force F-16s will be replaced. F-35As will be allotted to Air National Guard units, including the 114th FW; as production reaches sufficient numbers, F-35As will begin to replace many of the older fourth-generation aircraft, but the Air Force will continue to fly a mix of fifth- and fourth-generation fighters into the 2040s. This will allow the Air Force to maintain enough fighters to meet combatant commander requirements, provide the required training, and allow a reasonable and uninterrupted deployment tempo for the force. The Department of the Air Force selected the 115th Fighter Wing and the 187th Fighter Wing as the next Air National Guard locations to receive the F-35As, allowing a smooth transition into the next generation of air superiority.

One

World War II 1942–1946

Sioux Falls Joe Foss Field (current as of 2020), South Dakota, was established in 1937 as a civil airport. The City of Sioux Falls leased the airport to the US Army three months after the Japanese Imperial Navy aircraft carrier attack on US Navy and US Army installations at and around Pearl Harbor, Hawaii, on Sunday morning, December 7, 1941. The Sioux Falls war installation was named Sioux Falls Army Air Field. At Sioux Falls, the US Army Corps of Engineers developed a three-runway triangular layout (this pattern allowed continuous landings and takeoffs regardless of wind direction); work was conducted from 1942 to 1947. It became one of the many final aircrew training stops for those deploying overseas in the Boeing B-17 Flying Fortress and Consolidated B-24 Liberator bombers. Later in the war, Boeing B-29 Superfortress aircrews used the airbase for training before deploying to the Marianas Islands (Guam, Tinian, and Saipan) in the Pacific, assigned to the 20th Air Force to carry out the strategic bombing of the Japanese home islands. The airbase also supported the training of North American P-51D Mustang fighter pilots. Sioux Falls Army Air Field's primary function was as the US Army Air Forces Technical Training Command Radio Operators And Mechanics School from July 6, 1942, to May 11, 1945. The school trained radio operators and mechanics in radio and electrical fundamentals, how to take radio bearings and direction finding using triangulation, Ohm's Law and Morse code, and how to use Super Heterodyne receivers and other equipment.

This is a 1943 aerial photograph of Sioux Falls Army Air Field. It was the large World War II US Army Air Forces Technical Training Command Radio Operators And Mechanics School. The airfield had to be large enough to accommodate up to 28,000 officers, trainees, and staff. (Courtesy US Air Force Historical Research Agency.)

Seen here is a close-up oblique aerial photograph of Sioux Falls Army Air Field in 1943. The training classrooms' large rectangular buildings are on the left side of the photograph, and endless rows of barracks are to the right. (Courtesy US Air Force Historical Research Agency.)

This is a 1943 photograph taken during winter months, with snow on the ground, of the central area of Sioux Falls Army Air Field, with the base command flagpole and operations/headquarters building visible. (Courtesy the Siouxland Heritage Museum.)

The airfield base chapel was a modified barracks fitted with tall windows, an end-side double-entry door, and a traditional steeple above the door. A few of the airfield buildings are visible to the right background. The photograph was taken in 1946, when this was no longer an active training facility, as indicated by the weeds growing up in front of the chapel. (Courtesy the Siouxland Heritage Museum.)

Shown in this 1943 photograph are a few of the many identical barracks built at the Sioux Falls Army Air Field. The barracks were set on rows of spaced-out concrete foundation blocks, all-wood construction with 2-by-4 stud framing on a 24-inch center to save materials and cost, with shingles and tar paper external siding, single-pane glass, and heated by coal stoves. (Courtesy 114th Fighter Wing.)

This is a close-up, side-angle view of one of the many barracks on the Sioux Falls Army Air Field for the trainees attending the US Army Air Forces Technical Training Command Radio Operators and Mechanics School. These were temporary structures built to last for five to seven years—the War Department's estimated time to defeat Germany, Italy, and Japan by Allied forces during World War II. (Courtesy 114th Fighter Wing.)

The three buildings positioned close together, wider and longer than a standard barracks structure, in a central location probably are one location for the numerous mess halls to serve meals to airfield personnel and thousands of trainees. (Courtesy 114th Fighter Wing.)

Seen here is a view toward the Sioux Falls Army Air Field flight line with a large hangar in the background. The white single-story building is for operations of one of the US Army Air Forces Boeing B-17 Flying Fortress and Consolidated B-24 Liberator aircrew training squadrons (later transitioning in 1944 to Boeing B-29 Superfortress aircrew training). In the center-left of the photograph is a 1929–1932 car, reflecting that once the United States shifted from consumer production to full wartime production, the production of civilian vehicles stopped. (Courtesy 114th Fighter Wing.)

Shown is the 1942-constructed operations building (in which the headquarters staff was housed). Wood was the primary construction material during World War II, quick to build to meet the ever-growing demands of preparing and fighting a world war in Europe and the Pacific. (Courtesy 114th Fighter Wing.)

Here is a rear view of one of the airfield's aircraft hangars, with the building at the rear for storage of aircraft spare parts to maintain B-17, B-24, and B-29 flight training operations. (Courtesy 114th Fighter Wing.)

Pictured are rows of classrooms at the US Army Air Forces Technical Training Command Radio Operators and Mechanics School. (Courtesy 114th Fighter Wing.)

Seen here is the substantial brick 1942-constructed airfield control tower with a roof-mounted 360-degree view of the three runways, taxiways, and aircraft parking ramps to control the large volume of US Army Air Forces bomber training flights. Later, it was replaced by a modern Federal Aviation Agency multistory tower to control Joe Foss Field commercial and South Dakota Air National Guard flight operations. (Courtesy the Siouxland Heritage Museum.)

Large class sizes were common at the US Army Air Forces Technical Training Command Radio Operators and Mechanics School. Shown are students learning how to repair various radio equipment that was used by the Army Air Forces in the United States and overseas in combat theaters of operation. (Author's collection.)

This is a photograph of World War II radio equipment on which US Army Air Forces Technical Training Command Radio Operators and Mechanics School trainees learned to operate and repair. This equipment was collected and is on display in a small museum at the World War II Cut Bank Army Air Forces Base in northwest Montana. It was a satellite Boeing B-17 Flying Fortress training base for Great Falls Air Forces Base. Equipment is on display at the Cut Bank's Airmen Memorial Museum. (Author's collection.)

Shown is a large World War II electronic radio unit that was a portable airfield operations radio transmitter/receiver. It was used during training at the US Army Air Forces Technical Training Command Radio Operators and Mechanics School. It usually was loaded into the back of a jeep or two-wheel jeep-towed cargo trailer acting as a temporary airfield control vehicle. This system was designed for operations in combat zones from captured and damaged enemy airfields and from rough grass strips. This allowed air combat operations to continue if the enemy damaged permanent airstrips. The equipment is on display at the Cut Bank's Airmen Memorial Museum. (Author's collection.)

There also was a noncommissioned officers' school at the Sioux Falls Army Air Field. This photograph of a class at the school shows Caucasian and African American NCOs (noncommissioned officers). The US Army was not desegregated until the Korean War by Pres. Harry Truman. (Courtesy 114th Fighter Wing.)

After the Allied invasion of Normandy, France, the 387th Fighter Squadron forward deployed to a captured German Luftwaffe airfield at Azelle, France. Shown are squadron mechanics working in the open inside a heavily damaged former German Luftwaffe hangar in January 1944, with snow outside the unheated hangar. (Courtesy US Air Force Historical Research Agency Archives.)

This is a photograph of US Marine Corps pilot Capt. Joe Foss in the cockpit of his Grumman F-4F Wildcat fighter on Hendersen Air Field, Guadalcanal Island, at which time he shot down 26 Japanese aircraft, becoming the US military's top ace during this combat. (Courtesy US Marine Corps Archives.)

Two

North American F-51 Mustang 1946–1954

On September 18, 1947, the US Air Force became a separate military branch under the new Department of Defense, under the authorization of the National Security Act, passed by the US Congress. Air Guard leaders fought hard to acquire modern aircraft and upgraded facilities. On September 20, 1947, the South Dakota Air National Guard became part of the US Air Force. In 1947, the squadron received 25 North American F-51D Mustang fighters. Training to bring pilots up to operational capabilities sometimes became very exciting, since the 175th FS was based on a civilian airport. The 175th FS's first summer field training camp was held at the Sioux Falls Airport in June 1948, but it was not repeated there until 1961. In 1950, Pres. Harry Truman mobilized Air National Guard units to support the US forces fighting in South Korea after North Korea invaded the south, starting the Korean War. The 175th FIS was assigned to the 133rd FG, Minnesota Air National Guard, as an air defense unit to protect the continental United States. On March 2, 1951, the squadron was federalized and brought to active duty during the Korean War under the Air Defense Command but not deployed as an intact unit to the Far East Air Force for aerial combat in Korea. In August 1951, the squadron was assigned to Rapid City Air Force Base for air defense of the B-36D bombers of the 28th Bombardment Wing (BW), Strategic Air Command (SAC). It was never assigned to the Far East Air Force to fly combat missions in South Korea. After control of the 175th FIS was returned to the State of South Dakota and the squadron was reorganized, it was commanded by Lt. Col. Duane Corning, with Colonel Foss appointed as chief of staff of the South Dakota Air National Guard. The squadron was again equipped with F-51Ds, which it flew in 1954. During the Mustang era with the South Dakota Air National Guard, six pilots died in crashes.

Shown is a North American F-51D Mustang fighter with the South Dakota Air National Guard, 175th Fighter Interceptor Squadron, on Joe Foss Field, Sioux Falls, South Dakota. These are the original aircraft markings with the squadron coyote insignia. The nose of a second F-51D Mustang is visible to the right; in the background is the 1942-constructed control tower building. (Courtesy 114th Fighter Wing.)

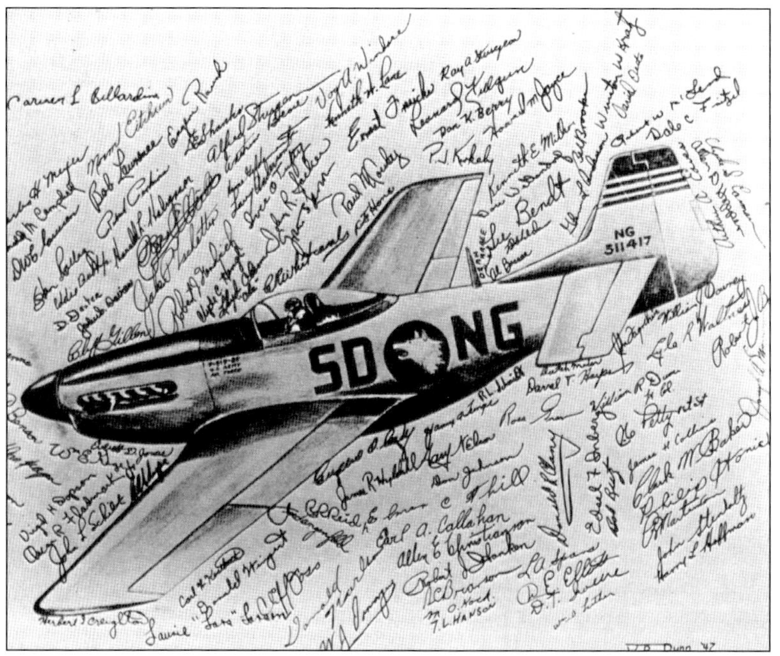

This is a 175th Fighter Interceptor Squadron member's drawing of a North American F-51D Mustang. The drawing was signed by the charter members of the 114th Fighter Wing, 175th Fighter Interceptor Squadron. (Courtesy 114th Fighter Wing.)

The 175th Fighter Interceptor Squadron remarked its North American F-51D Mustangs with standard US Air Force markings. The ground crewman on the left wing of the F-51D in the background is working on the maintenance post-flight write-up before the next flight. (Courtesy 114th Fighter Wing.)

Three North American F-51D Mustangs are on the 175th Fighter Squadron flight line with their cockpit canopies open. The Mustang during World War II and the postwar time frame was the US Air Forces' most high-performance piston-engine fighter. (Courtesy 114th Fighter Wing.)

Maintenance crewmen work on the open engine cowling of a North American F-51D Mustang on the 175th Fighter Interceptor Squadron flight line, with other North American F-51D Mustangs visible to either side. (Courtesy 114th Fighter Wing.)

Pictured is a line of three North American F-51D Mustangs on the 175th Fighter Interceptor Squadron flight line with pilots in cockpits and crew and maintenance crewmen performing operational checks/inspections on the aircraft. (Courtesy 114th Fighter Wing.)

Here is a group photograph of aircraft ground crewmen (mechanics) in front of and on the left wing of a North American F-51D Mustang on the 175th Fighter Interceptor Squadron flight line. (Courtesy 114th Fighter Wing.)

This is a photograph of 114th Fighter Interceptor Group, 175th Fighter Interceptor Squadron personnel in front of a North American F-51D Mustang at Camp Casper, Wyoming, during their first deployment for summer field training at this location. (Courtesy South Dakota National Guard.)

Shown is the 175th Fighter Interceptor Squadron flight line with a North American F-51D Mustang, cockpit open, and one of the squadron members' convertible parked along the right side of the fighter. This is no longer permitted after the terrorist attacks on the United States on September 11, 2001. (Courtesy South Dakota National Guard.)

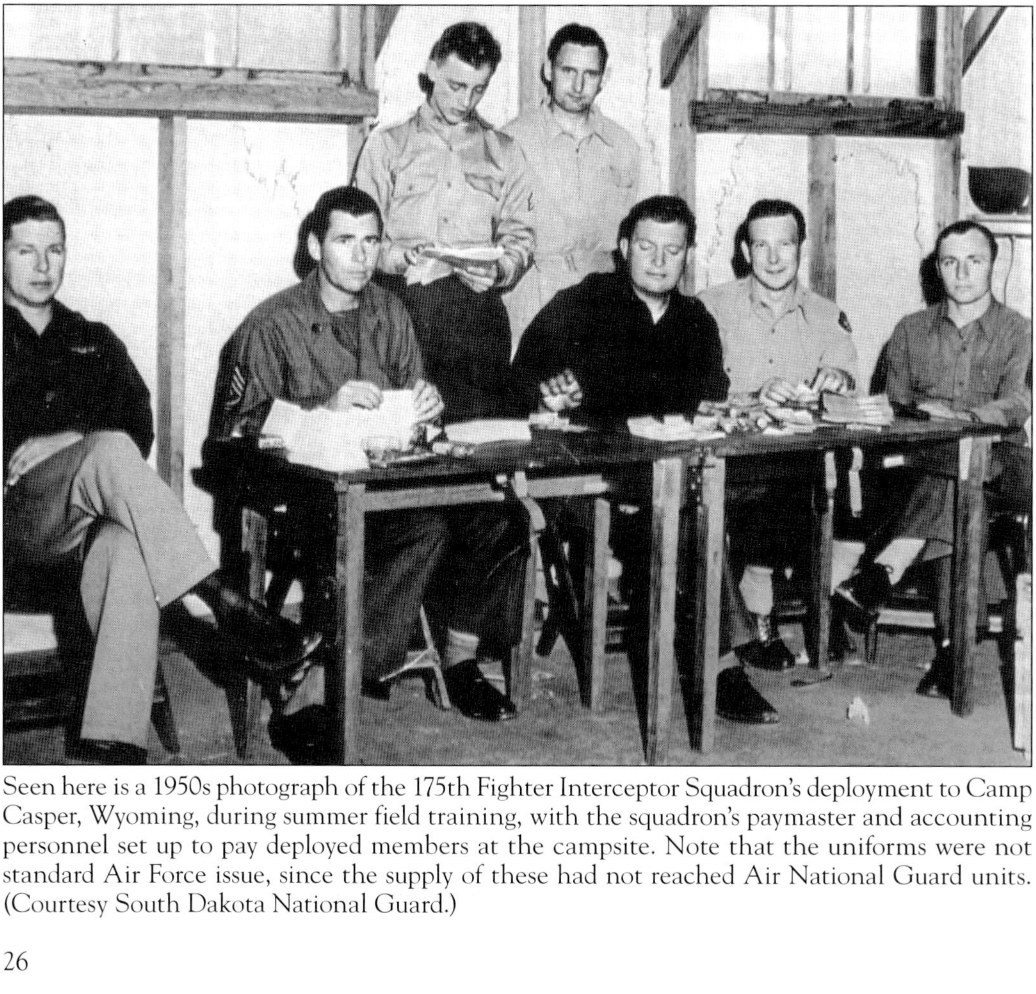

Seen here is a 1950s photograph of the 175th Fighter Interceptor Squadron's deployment to Camp Casper, Wyoming, during summer field training, with the squadron's paymaster and accounting personnel set up to pay deployed members at the campsite. Note that the uniforms were not standard Air Force issue, since the supply of these had not reached Air National Guard units. (Courtesy South Dakota National Guard.)

Here is a photograph of the 175th Fighter Interceptor Squadron holding its first open house on Air Force Day, September 18, 1947. Visitors look into the cockpit of a North American F-51D Mustang in the maintenance hangar while a local Sioux Falls band plays music. (Courtesy 114th Fighter Wing.)

Seen here is a March 1949 photograph of a 114th Fighter Interceptor Group, South Dakota Air National Guard recruiting event. A North American F-51D Mustang was trucked to a downtown Sioux Falls used car dealership on Tenth and North Main Streets for display. (Courtesy 114th Fighter Wing.)

This is a photograph of North American F-51D Mustangs inside the 175th Fighter Interceptor Squadron maintenance hangar. If ground crew personnel carefully and slowly pushed the Mustangs inside, the hangar could store many and keep them safe from possible hail storm damage, which frequently occurred from May to September in South Dakota. In the foreground is a North American T-6 Texan trainer. (Courtesy 114th Fighter Wing.)

One of the 114th Fighter Interceptor Group's air defense missions was to protect Strategic Air Command's 28th Bombardment Wing's Convair B-36D Peacemaker intercontinental strategic nuclear bombers on Ellsworth Air Force Base to the west at Rapid City, South Dakota. (Author's collection.)

Three

Lockheed F-94 Starfire 1954–1958

The turbojet age arrived at the South Dakota Air National Guard in June 1954 with the delivery of the Lockheed F-94A and B Starfires and the Lockheed T-33A Shooting Star transition pilot trainer. The F-94 was a two-man aircraft with the pilot in the front seat and the radar operator in the back seat. It did not take too long for the 175th FIS pilots to be checked out in the F-94, aided by training in the T-33A. On August 15, 1954, the squadron was ordered to provide two F-94s, five pilots, and five radar operators to participate in the active air defense of the continental United States because of a possible growing threat by the Soviet Union of a nuclear attack.

In April 1956, the South Dakota Air National Guard underwent a reorganization, redesignated as the 114th Fighter Interceptor Group (air defense). The 114th FIG consisted of the 175th FIS, 114th Air Base Squadron, dispensary, material squadron, and headquarters of the 114th FG. The 114th FG moved from the piston era to that of the turbojet with the arrival of the F-94. The squadron was upgraded to the F-94C, classified as an all-weather, unguided-rocket-firing fighter-interceptor with a drogue chute to slow the aircraft's speed on the runway after landing. Initially, the 114th FIG held its drills every Thursday night for two hours. Drills then changed to the weekends in 1957: 1300–2100 on Saturdays and 0800–1430 on Sundays. Until 1957, most of the military indoctrination training was held at Joe Foss Field. With a mix of prior service and non–prior service personnel, this was somewhat successful. In 1957, the first group of personnel from the South Dakota Air National Guard required to go to basic military training traveled by the group's C-47 to San Antonio, Texas, returning after completing training by passenger rail service to Sioux Falls. The 175th Fighter Interceptor Squadron flew approximately 4,000 hours in the F-94C, receiving numerous national awards in 1957.

The Lockheed T-33 Shooting Star was assigned to the 175th Fighter Interceptor Squadron initially as a transition trainer from the piston-engine North American F-51D Mustang to the South Dakota Air National Guard's first turbojet fighter, the Lockheed F-94 Starfighter. The aircraft is shown on the squadron's flight line. (Courtesy South Dakota National Guard.)

This is a static display of Lockheed T-33 Shooting Star instruments and cockpit equipment, now on display at the South Dakota National Guard Museum. (Author's collection.)

The Lockheed T-33 Shooting Star cockpit center pilot's console is pictured here on display at the South Dakota National Guard Museum. To the left is a T-33 ejection seat, and to the right is a Vought A-7D Corsair II ejection seat. (Author's collection.)

Shown are two Lockheed F-94 Starfires in formation over Joe Foss Field, photographed from a third F-94, during a 175th Fighter Interceptor Squadron formation training flight. (Courtesy 114th Fighter Wing.)

Shown are two 175th Fighter Interceptor Squadron Lockheed F-94 Starfires on the flight line, canopies closed, with nose radars covered with tarps for protection from blowing debris and weather. The pilot sat in the front cockpit seat, and the radar observer was in the rear cockpit seat. (Courtesy 114th Fighter Wing.)

Here is a close-up view of the left forward fuselage section of the Lockheed F-94 Starfire, with the cockpit canopy open and crew access ladder in position below the open cockpit. (Courtesy 114th Fighter Wing.)

A Lockheed F-94 Starfire is on display at the National Museum of the US Air Force. The F-94 was equipped with wingtip fuel tanks for extended aerial interception range. Starting with the 100th production aircraft and retrofitted on previous aircraft, rocket pods were mounted to the leading edge on each wing. Each held 12 unguided (folding-fin) 2.75-inch rockets, supplementing the 24 mounted around an internal compartment in the nose. (Courtesy Museum of the US Air Force.)

This is a photograph of Col. Joseph Foss on the ladder into the cockpit of a Lockheed F-94 Starfire on the 175th Fighter Interceptor Squadron flight line. (Courtesy South Dakota National Guard.)

The flight line of the 175th Fighter Interceptor Squadron is seen here with its complement of Lockheed F-94 Starfires. The aircrews of two Starfires are preparing to launch on a training mission. (Courtesy 114th Fighter Wing.)

The Russian Air Force threat to the United States, which the 175th Fighter Squadron might encounter in its air defense role, was the Myasischev Mya-4 Bison, a four-turbojet-engine intercontinental strategic nuclear bomber. It was the Soviet Union's copy of the Strategic Air Command's Boeing B-52 Stratofortress bomber, but it was never produced in the same numbers as the B-52. (Courtesy US Air Force.)

Shown is the Russian Air Force Tupolev Tu-95 Bear, a four-turboprop-engine intercontinental nuclear bomber, which was the replacement for the Mya-4 bomber. Like the US Air Force B-52H Stratofortress bomber, it remains operational. (Courtesy US Air Force.)

Pictured is the 175th Fighter Interceptor Squadron maintenance hangar, building No. 40, with Lockheed F-94s in the process of inspection and maintenance or modifications as directed by Lockheed Aircraft. (Courtesy 114th Fighter Wing.)

Two Lockheed F-94 Starfire airframe mechanics work on the removed tail section of the aircraft, repairing structural rivets identified as needing replacement. (Courtesy South Dakota National Guard.)

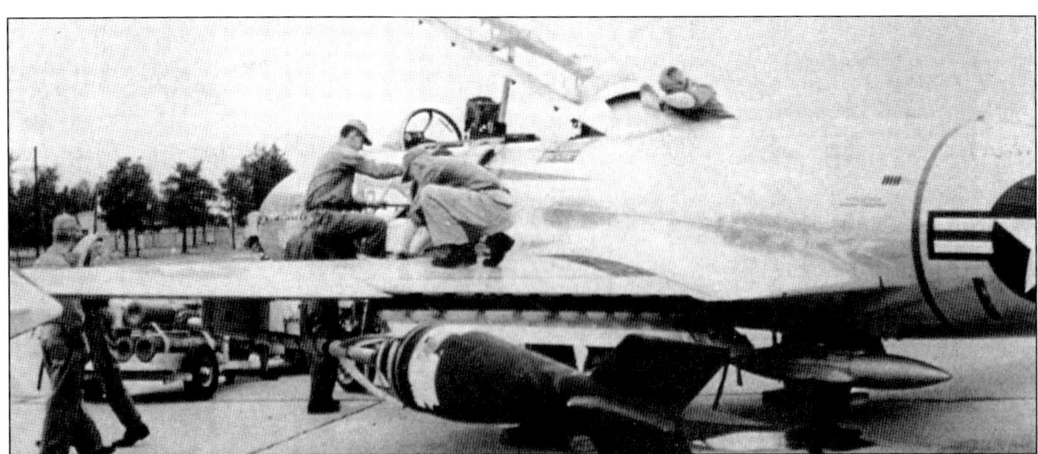

For aerial rocket firing practice, a Lockheed T-33 Shooting Star is prepared, carrying a Delmar Tow Target. Once airborne, the tow target will be released behind the aircraft to a distance of 5,000 feet. This provided F-94 aircrews aerial target practice. (Courtesy South Dakota National Guard.)

From left to right are Maj. Gen. Duane L. "Duke" Corning and Brig. Gen. Joseph J. "Joe" Foss, cofounders of the South Dakota Air National Guard, who became leaders in the state's National Guard. (Courtesy South Dakota National Guard.)

During winter, two Lockheed F-94 Starfires are parked on the snow-covered flight line. In South Dakota, the winter months can bring very cold temperatures, wind, and snow, sometimes reaching blizzard conditions. (Courtesy 114th Fighter Wing.)

Four Lockheed F-94 Starfires are pictured on the 175th Fighter Interceptor Squadron flight line. (Courtesy 114th Fighter Wing.)

This photograph shows attempts to clear snow from the Lockheed F-94 Starfire parking areas, with a road grader in the left background clearing the runway. It is interesting to note that the World War II control tower is visible to the left of the runway. (Courtesy 114th Fighter Wing.)

Hangar doors in these photographs are open, with Lockheed F-94 Starfires in the process of inspection and maintenance or modifications as directed by Lockheed Aircraft. (Both, courtesy 114th Fighter Wing.)

Ground crew personnel are in front of a Lockheed F-94 Starfire on the 175th Fighter Interceptor Squadron flight line. (Courtesy 114th Fighter Wing.)

Two Lockheed F-94 Starfires, with markings of the South Dakota Air National Guard, 114th Fighter Wing, 175th Fighter Squadron, are airborne on a local training flight. This photograph was taken from an adjacent F-94. (Courtesy 114th Fighter Wing.)

Four

Northrop F-89 Scorpion 1958–1961

The Northrop F-89D and F-89J Scorpion brought the South Dakota Air National Guard into the forefront of air defense of the continental United States during the Cold War due to a possible Russian Air Force bomber attack with nuclear weapons. The Scorpion was a two-man, all-weather interceptor that could shoot down Russian Air Force bombers penetrating US airspace. A training team was sent by the Air Force to Joe Foss Field on April 7, 1958, to train the squadron's mechanics and technicians on the F-89 Scorpion. Pilots and radar operators were trained in night classes at the squadron. The Scorpion required a higher degree of expertise than the F-94C Starfire. More technicians were required, because the Scorpion's twin Allison J-35 turbojet engines were mounted close to the ground, which often sucked in debris, causing foreign object damage (FOD), requiring continual engine inspection and repairs as needed. The Scorpion had internal fuel cells that had to be removed to check for leaks. There was only one hangar available to do this maintenance work, and removing the fuel cells resulted in aviation fuel leaking onto the hangar's floor, with the resulting fumes creating a possible fire danger and personnel exposure to toxic fumes. The 114th Fighter Interceptor Group received funds to build a new headquarters, building No. 60. The deactivation of the 114th Material Squadron, then the forming of the 114th Consolidated Aircraft Maintenance Squadron (CAMRON), created more changes. Mechanics were reassigned from the 175th Fighter Interceptor Squadron to CAMRON, leaving the 175th Fighter Interceptor Squadron as a tactical squadron. Summer field training camps were held at Camp Wisconsin and Alpena, Michigan. After 1960, the 114th FIG initiated the "Texas style" of competition at these training camps. Rather than travel with the unit to training, individual members were given the option to schedule their own active duty period and perform it in Sioux Falls.

This is a view of a 54th Fighter Interceptor Squadron Northrop F-89J Scorpion in front of an alert hangar on Ellsworth Air Force Base. The alert hangar has two doors; the rear door allows the aircraft to head straight in and become cocked for an alert launch, going directly out the open front hangar door, onto the taxiway, and then taking off on the runway. The four alert hangars were eventually moved from the end of the runway to the current location for the South Dakota Air and Space Museum indoor display areas, museum store, and administration. (Courtesy South Dakota Air and Space Museum.)

An F-89 is airborne over farmland of eastern South Dakota in this photograph, taken from an adjacent F-89 during the training flight. (Courtesy 114th Fighter Wing.)

A 175th Fighter Interceptor Squadron crew is pictured here during what was described as a "hot" landing, when the pilot ran off the end of the runway in his F-89. It came to a stop off the runway without damaging its landing gear. A tow vehicle is attached to the dual rear landing gears and slowly is pulling the aircraft back onto the runway as ground crewmen keep the nose landing gear lined up straight. Once the F-89 was back on the runway, it was towed to a maintenance hangar to inspect possible damage to the aircraft. (Courtesy 114th Fighter Wing.)

A mix of F-89Ds and F-89Js are on the 175th Fighter Interceptor Squadron flight line. The F-89Js did not have rocket pods, since their armament was mounted on under-wing pylons for conventional air-to-air missiles and two Genie unguided nuclear-warhead rockets. (Courtesy 114th Fighter Wing.)

Shown is a row of F-89Ds on the flight line. This is a close-up view of a power-starting generator alongside the front F-89D as well as fire extinguishers in ready in case there was an engine fire during startup. (Courtesy 114th Fighter Wing.)

Pictured is an F-89D Scorpion on the 175th Fighter Interceptor Squadron flight line. (Courtesy 114th Fighter Wing.)

Seen here is an F-89D with an open cockpit. The pilot is visible in the front cockpit as he taxis out onto the taxiway and then onto the runway for takeoff on a training flight. (Courtesy 114th Fighter Wing.)

Pictured is a clean version of a Northrop F-89 Scorpion at the Northrop factory, showing the clean lines of the aircraft used for test flight evaluations. (Courtesy US Air Force.)

In this close-up photograph is the right wing of an F-89D Scorpion with the rocket pod cover removed, showing the warheads of the 2.75-inch folding-fin rockets and the center-mounted larger 5.9-inch high-velocity rockets. (Courtesy 114th Fighter Wing.)

This is a 1959 photograph of an F-89D on the 175th Fighter Interceptor Squadron flight line. In the front cockpit position is Lieutenant Costain. Radar observer Lieutenant Kittelson is getting up off his seat in the rear cockpit position to climb out and down the access ladder on the side of the aircraft. (Courtesy South Dakota National Guard.)

A Northrop F-89J Scorpion is on static display on Dyess Air Force Base, Texas. The F-89J was capable of carrying two Genie nuclear-warhead unguided air-to-air anti-aircraft rockets. (Author's collection.)

This is a photograph of the Hughes AMM-4 Falcon air-to-air missile, operational with the US Air Force starting in 1956. It was in two variants: GAR-1, a semi-active homing, radar-guided missile, and GAR-2, a heat-seeking missile. It is on display in the South Dakota Air and Space Museum indoor display area. (Author's collection.)

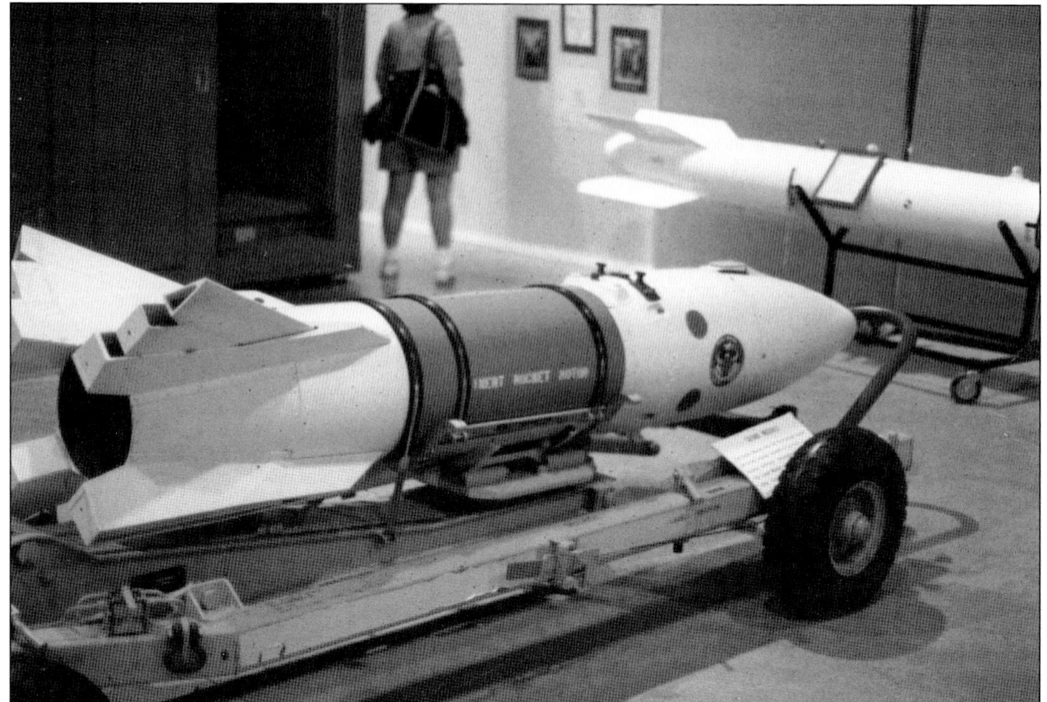

Shown is an inert training Genie air-to-air unguided rocket on its transporter and loader. It was used for the training of munitions personnel, security forces, maintenance, and flight personnel. Its training electronics mirrored that of an operational rocket. It is on display in the South Dakota Air and Space Museum indoor display area. (Author's collection.)

A Northrop F-89 Scorpion, at the head of a row of Scorpion fighters, is being refueled from a fuel truck. It was later replaced by a hydrant refueling system, a safer mode of refueling an aircraft on the flight line. (Author's collection.)

Five

Convair F-102 Delta Dagger 1960–1970

The 114th Fighter Interceptor Group upgraded to the Convair supersonic F-102A Delta Dagger, nicknamed "Duce." It was the US Air Force's first supersonic delta-wing fighter. The South Dakota Air National Guard began a four-aircraft, five-minute ready-launch alert to intercept unidentified aircraft and destroy possible hostile airborne targets. Conversion from the F-89 to the F-102 required intense training, starting with aircrew chiefs who went to Kelly Air Force Base, Texas. The 175th Fighter Interceptor Squadron was also equipped with a Convair TF-102, a side-by-side pilot conversion trainer, to upgrade to the high-performance, supersonic fighter.

The State of South Dakota approved distinctive National Guard license plates in 1963. In 1965, a new barracks, building No. 61, was completed with an open bay for officers and a second for enlisted. The building also contained the data, finance, and contracting units and was later modified into a club and small base exchange.

In 1966, Col. Justin Berger became the 114th Fighter Interceptor Group's new commander. In 1968, the "Palace Alert" program began, with six group fighter pilots volunteering. Its purpose was to relieve pilots in Europe and the South Pacific for tours of duty, serving up to 180 days. On Joe Foss Field, a new air defense alert ramp was completed, allowing the initiation of a 24-hour ready-launch alert program.

In 1969, the 114th Fighter Interceptor Group underwent a tactical evaluation and general inspection; the minimum passing score was 90 percent F-102 interception rate. The 114th Fighter Interceptor Group received a high rating, which is earned by only a minority of Air Force and Air Guard units. Recognition was again given to the South Dakota Air National Guard when it received the Aerospace Defense Command "A" Award in January 1970 for the sustained operational effectiveness of an exceptionally high degree. This recognition was given only to an elite few, and the South Dakota National Guard was proud to be among them. Tragically, during the F-102 period with the South Dakota Air National Guard, one pilot was killed: Capt. Joseph Eken.

This Convair F-102 Delta Dagger was flown by the 175th Fighter Interceptor Squadron. After decommissioning, it was acquired from Holloman Air Force Base, New Mexico, trucked to the South Dakota Air and Space Museum, Ellsworth Air Force Base, restored, and placed on outdoor display at the museum. (Author's collection.)

An F-102 is shown on display at Ellsworth Air Force Base during an open house after being restored by volunteers from the South Dakota Air and Space Museum. (Author's collection.)

This is an interesting photograph after an F-102 pilot made the wrong turn off the taxiway onto the main vehicle access road into and out of the flight line. The aircraft had to be towed back to the operational flight line. (Author's collection.)

A pilot is in the F-102 cockpit, with the crew chief on the access ladder, climbing back to the ground after helping the pilot secure himself into the cockpit. (Courtesy 114th Fighter Wing.)

The South Dakota National Guard never had a permanent ready-alert facility. Periodically, as shown in this photograph, two F-102s are on ready-launch alert, with pilots and ground crew running to the aircraft. This was training for alert aircraft, if authorized, to launch as soon as possible. (Courtesy 114th Fighter Wing.)

Two F-102s are airborne in formation. This photograph was taken from a third airborne F-102 from the 175th Fighter Interceptor Squadron. (Courtesy 114th Fighter Wing.)

This is a close-up photograph of the right-side view of an F-102 with the cockpit canopy open on the 175th Fighter Interceptor Squadron flight line. The operations building is in the background. (Courtesy 114th Fighter Wing.)

Pictured is a heavy-lift helicopter with an F-102 slung below being transported to a position in the 114th Fighter Interceptor Group airpark (at that time). (Courtesy 114th Fighter Wing.)

The conversion to the supersonic Convair F-102 Delta Dagger required new and specialized flight and ground training. Shown in this November 1960 photograph is a group of 175th Fighter Interceptor Squadron crew chiefs in front of a Texas Air National Guard F-102 at Kelly Air Force Base, Texas. (Courtesy South Dakota National Guard.)

Shown are the side-by-side instructor (right) and pilot transition student seats (left). The bulge along the front of the TF-102 aircraft allows room for the dual-pilot configuration. (Courtesy US Air Force.)

A pilot (left) and crew chief (right) are in front of a Convair F-102 Delta Dagger on the 175th Fighter Interceptor Squadron flight line. (Courtesy 114th Fighter Wing.)

This is a close-up view of a TF-102 transition trainer with side-by-side seating for an instructor in the left seat and a student pilot in the right for supersonic flight training. (Courtesy US Air Force.)

Seen here is a row of F-102s on the 175th Fighter Interceptor Squadron flight line. There were not enough aircraft hangars for covered parking, with most aircraft parked in the open on the flight line. (Courtesy 114th Fighter Wing.)

Seen here is a photograph of the left side of an F-102 wearing the "S. Dak. Air Guard" fuselage markings. (Courtesy 114th Fighter Wing.)

Six

North American F-100D Super Sabre 1970–1977

By the time the 114th FG began transitioning to the North American F-100D Super Sabre, the South Dakota Air National Guard had implemented several operational upgrades. Another significant change came in May 1970, when the 114th FG, Aerospace Defense Command, the South Dakota Air National Guard unit, was redesignated the 114th TFG, under Tactical Air Command. The 175th Fighter Squadron was redesignated as the 175th TFS. The 114th TFG strength increased to 800 personnel and the facility to 33 buildings on 133 acres of land at the south end of the airport. Construction started on a new aircraft maintenance building and motor pool. Training changed to weekend unit training assemblies (UTAs). It was equipped with a two-seat TF-100F trainer. With the F-100D arrival, the group transitioned from an air defense role to that of ground support. From 1972 to 1974, the South Dakota Air National Guard saw the final four Lockheed T-33A Shooting Star trainers takeoff from Joe Foss Field. The F-100D era came to an end in March 1976, when the 114th TFG began receiving the Convair A-7D Corsair II. The last four F-100Ds assigned to the 114th TFG took off from Joe Foss Field on June 4, 1977. Pilots assigned to the 114th TFG flew these four F-100Ds to Iskashir, Turkey, where they were transferred to the Turkish Air Force. One of the 114th TFG's, aircraft serial number 55-3754, had been flown by the US Air Force Thunderbirds, 1964–1967, and then by the 114th TFG from 1970 to 1977. The aircraft was painted to match that of the Thunderbirds to make its final historic flight, flying in formation with the Thunderbirds. It was then flown to the National Museum of the US Air Force, Wright-Patterson Air Force Base at Dayton, Ohio, where it is currently on display. The balance of the Air Guard's F-100Ds was flown to the 309th Aerospace Maintenance and Regeneration Group (2020 name), Air Force Material Command, for storage. On June 25, 1970, Capt. Rodney Madison died in an F-100D crash.

This North American F-100D Super Sabre, with Vietnam War green jungle camouflage colors, was transferred from active-duty US Air Force combat squadrons to the South Dakota Air National Guard. It was modified with a right-wing-mounted aerial refueling probe for extended combat missions. (Courtesy 114th Fighter Wing.)

Shown is an F-100D on display at the South Dakota Air National Guard, 114th Fighter Wing Air Park. (Courtesy 114th Fighter Wing.)

This North American F-100D Super Sabre is on display at the South Dakota Air and Space Museum, positioned in front of a former Air Defense Command ready aircraft alert hangar bay, one of four such bays formerly on Ellsworth Air Force Base. The alert facility was moved from the end of the Ellsworth runway to its current location outside the main gate to the base, where it is used as an interior display space, museum store, and administration offices. (Author's collection.)

This is a squadron group photograph of F-100D pilots assigned to the 175th Tactical Fighter Squadron for the South Dakota Air National Guard. (Courtesy 114th Fighter Wing.)

A ground crewman is pictured in front of an F-100D holding a wind-speed meter to calculate ramp air winds. (Courtesy 114th Fighter Wing.)

Seen here is an F-100D landing at an air defense runway with a drogue parachute deployed to slow the forward landing roll of the aircraft to taxing speed. At that time, the parachute will be released for recovery by ground crew personnel. (Courtesy 114th Fighter Wing.)

This is a transitional photograph showing the replacement of the F-100D in the foreground with the Vought A-7D Corsair II in the background approaching the parking ramp. (Courtesy 114th Fighter Wing.)

Winter weather in South Dakota can consist of heavy snowfalls and blizzard conditions. The F-100D is surrounded by a pile of snow pushed off the parking ramp. (Courtesy 114th Fighter Wing.)

Four 175th Tactical Fighter Squadron F-100Ds are pictured in formation above and south of Mount Rushmore Memorial. This photograph was taken from an adjacent F-100D. (Courtesy 114th Fighter Wing.)

An F-100D flies over the snow-covered Black Hills of western South Dakota in an image captured from an adjacent F-100D. (Courtesy 114th Fighter Wing.)

Shown is a pilot inside the open cockpit of an F-100D getting ready to start the engine for a training flight, assisted by three ground crewmen. (Courtesy 114th Fighter Wing.)

A North American F-100D Super Sabre is on the flight line, with the pilot in the cockpit. The engine just started, as noted by the heavy smoke from the engine exhaust. (Courtesy 114th Fighter Wing.)

This F-100D is airborne on a training flight, showing its clean lines in a photograph taken from an adjacent F-100D. (Courtesy 114th Fighter Wing.)

This close-up view is of the right wing of an F-100D with the aerial refueling probe, angled up off the wing to allow a clean airborne connection with the refueling receptacle on an aerial tanker. This photograph was taken from an adjacent F-100D. (Courtesy 114th Fighter Wing.)

Seven

Vought A-7D Corsair II 1977–1991

The 114th TFG received the Vought A-7D Corsair II in March 1977. The A-7D was a single-seat fighter designed for close air support of US ground forces. A two-seat Convair A-7K Corsair was flown as a trainer and instructor check ride of the pilots. In 1986, the 114th TFG finished first among A-7D units, achieving flying 5,397 accident-free hours. By the end of the year, the group had flown 14,287 hours with no FOD incidents. During September 1986, several 114th TFG personnel were assigned to support the visit by Pres. Ronald Reagan to Joe Foss Field and Sioux Falls. The 114th Resource Protection Team augmented local police units to assist in the protection of the president. In 1988, the 114th Tactical Fighter Group made a historic Checkered Flag deployment to St. Truiden, Belgium. The 114th Tactical Fighter Group was the first Air Force combat air unit to operate out of Belgium since the end of World War II. On August 12–13, 1989, the City of Sioux Falls and the South Dakota Air National Guard cosponsored Airshow 89 with the theme "Parade of Flight." The air show was part of the South Dakota centennial celebration. The 114th Tactical Fighter Group repainted one of its A-7Ds white with red and blue accent markings, naming it the *Spirit of South Dakota*. The aircraft was flown during this air show and then at other air shows to honor the 100th birthday of the state of South Dakota. In 1990, the 114th TFG was informed that it would be replacing its Vought A-7D Corsair IIs with the General Dynamics F-16C Fighting Falcon, a frontline Air Force fighter with many different operational capabilities. To maintain a historical tie to the past, the 114th TFG arranged for the transfer of a Lockheed T-33A Shooting Star from the desert storage area at the Aerospace Maintenance Regeneration Center at Davis-Monthan Air Force Base. The T-33A was restored and placed on display along Industrial Avenue.

A Vought A-7D Corsair II is shown making a low-level pass over the runway at Joe Foss Field with landing gear down. The engine intake is visible below the nose and cockpit. Three underwing weapon pylons are visible under the right wing. Flaps are extended to maintain control at near-landing speed. (Courtesy 114th Fighter Wing.)

The right side of a Vought A-7D Corsair II is painted in Southeast Asia green and tan camouflage. This paint scheme was intended to make it more difficult for Viet Cong and North Vietnamese Army units to identify any approaching A-7D attacks during ground-support missions for US and South Vietnamese forces. The A-7Ds for the South Dakota Air National Guard were pulled from US Air Force combat squadrons for transfer to the South Dakota and other Air National Guard units. (Courtesy 114th Fighter Wing.)

This is a 1991 transitional photograph of an airborne A-7D in the foreground, and its replacement, the General Dynamics F-16 Fighting Falcon, is in the background. (Courtesy 114th Fighter Wing.)

An A-7D Corsair II is on the flight line with F-100Ds during the transition to the A-7D. The pilot is in the cockpit pending takeoff on a training flight. (Courtesy 114th Fighter Wing.)

This is a head-on view of a 175th Tactical Fighter Squadron A-7D on the airfield during Operation Coronet Stone in 1988, a Checkered Flag training deployment to St. Truiden, Belgium. This South Dakota Air National Guard aircraft was part of the first US Air Force unit to operate out of Belgium since the US Army Air Forces during World War II. (Courtesy 114th Fighter Wing.)

This 175th Tactical Fighter Squadron A-7D flies over the southern Black Hills, near Mount Rushmore Memorial, during a cross-state training flight. (Courtesy 114th Fighter Wing.)

For long-distance (especially overseas) deployments, this photograph shows one of four A-7Ds hooked to the Boeing "flying boom" aerial refueling probe from the rear of a Boeing KC-135A Stratotanker. (Courtesy 114th Fighter Wing.)

Shown is a long row of A-7Ds with members of the 175th Tactical Fighter Squadron posing for a group photograph. (Courtesy 114th Fighter Wing.)

This former 175th Tactical Fighter Squadron Vought A-7D Corsair II is on display at the South Dakota Air and Space Museum. (Author's collection.)

Four 175th Tactical Fighter Squadron A-7Ds are in a line formation flying above and to the south of Mount Rushmore Memorial in this image captured from an adjacent A-7D. (Courtesy 114th Fighter Wing.)

This is a transition photograph of a Vought A-7D Corsair II in the foreground with its replacement flying alongside, the General Dynamics F-16 Fighting Falcon. (Courtesy 114th Fighter Wing.)

An A-7D begins a takeoff for a training flight from Joe Foss Field to maintain pilot proficiency. (Courtesy 114th Fighter Wing.)

This is a left-side photograph of a Vought A-7D Corsair II, with a camouflage paint scheme, carrying extended range fuel tanks. (Courtesy 114th Fighter Wing.)

A Vought A-7K Corsair II pilot trainer, with dual cockpit controls, is parked at the head of a row of A-7Ds at the 132nd Tactical Fighter Wing, Iowa Air National Guard, at the Des Moines International Airport. This aircraft was also flown by the 175th Tactical Fighter Squadron. (Courtesy 114th Fighter Wing.)

Pictured here is a Vought A-7D Corsair II with a green and tan camouflage paint scheme. The aircraft, formerly flown by the 175th Fighter Wing, Maryland Air National Guard, is on display at the National Museum of the US Air Force. (Courtesy National Museum of the US Air Force.)

Shown is a row of A-7Ds of the 175th Tactical Fighter Squadron parked outside on the flight line for this public affairs photograph of the fighter aircraft. (Courtesy 114th Fighter Wing.)

Deployed personnel of the 114th Tactical Fighter Group are pictured in front of four Vought A-7D Corsair IIs on December 23, 1989, at Howard Air Force Base, Panama. The deployment was in support of Operation Just Cause. (Courtesy 114th Fighter Wing.)

This is a right-side photograph of a former 175th Tactical Fighter Squadron A-7D on display at the South Dakota National Guard Museum. The aircraft was painted red, white, and blue and marked as *Spirit of South Dakota*. This one-of-a-kind 175th Tactical Fighter Squadron A-7D took part in the August 12–13, 1989, air show marking the State of South Dakota's centennial celebration and was then repainted in traditional colors. (Author's collection.)

Eight

General Dynamics F-16 Fighting Falcon 1991–Present

The first three General Dynamics F-16 Fighting Falcons (two C variants and one D variant—a two-seat transition trainer with other options) landed at Joe Foss Field on August 14, 1991, to the cheers of state and local VIPs, Air Guard personnel, and their families. Since the South Dakota Air National Guard was converting from the A-7D to the F-16C, it was not mission-capable during the process and therefore not available for unit call up for Operation Desert Storm, which kicked off with a massive air attack on Iraq on January 16, 1991. To make the conversion and transition successful, prior to the conversion date, several pilots attended transition training while Air Guard members trained for the new aircraft at Joe Foss Field. On January 18, 1992, a 114th TFG team deployed to Ramstein Air Force Base, Germany, to begin accepting F-16Cs, returning to Joe Foss Field on February 21. A second team was deployed back to Germany on February 21, completing aircraft acceptance on March 29, 1992. The group's first NATO deployment with the F-16C was back to St. Truiden Air Base, Belgium. Eight F-16Cs completed a nine-hour flight with air refueling to Belgium. During the deployment mission, the capable rate was 94 percent. On October 1, 1995, the unit was redesignated as the 114th FW. Following the September 11, 2001, terrorist attack on America, the 114th FW immediately began to experience involuntary, but expected, federal activations of wing personnel. By 2010, conversion from Block 30 F-16Cs to Block 40 F-16Cs started, completed by 2012. These F-16Cs came from Hill Air Force Base, Utah. On March 18, 2020, during the COVID-19 Coronavirus pandemic crisis, the 114th FW at Joe Foss Field restricted base access to current unit members and for official business only. These restrictions were necessary to preserve fore readiness while limiting the continuing spread of COVID-19 and to preserve the health and welfare of the 114th FW service members, their families, and the local community in which they live.

Seen here is a photo montage of the first three General Dynamics F-16s (two C variants and one D variant, the two-seat trainer) after the aircraft landed at Joe Foss Field as part of the welcoming ceremony at the 114th Tactical Fighter Group on August 14, 1991. The 114th Tactical Fighter Group was redesignated the 114th Fighter Wing in October 1995. (Courtesy 114th Fighter Wing.)

This image was captured of the main vehicle access gate when the South Dakota Air National Guard unit was designated the 114th Fighter Group. (Courtesy 114th Fighter Wing.)

An F-16 is shown after takeoff, with its landing gear nearly retracted into the fuselage, for a local training flight then touch-and-go landing/takeoffs for practice. (Courtesy 114th Fighter Wing.)

In this photograph, an F-16 is over wind farm electric generators as it has landing gear down on its approach to Joe Foss Field. (Courtesy 114th Fighter Wing.)

Three F-16s are on the 175th Fighter Squadron flight line with pilots inside the closed cockpits and ground personnel assisting in the engine starts prior to a training flight. (Courtesy 114th Fighter Wing.)

An F-16 is on the flight line with the pilot in the closed canopy and the ground crewman completing the final aircraft check prior to releasing the aircraft for taxiing to the runway and taking off for a training flight. (Courtesy 114th Fighter Wing.)

A 175th Fighter Squadron F-16 with landing gear down is shown over the Joe Foss Field runway. (Courtesy 114th Fighter Wing.)

An F-16 waits on the taxiway as a McDonnell Douglas C-17 Globemaster III lands on the runway. The F-16 from the 175th Fighter Squadron was deployed to an Air Force base for operational bombing training. (Courtesy 114th Fighter Wing.)

An F-16 is pictured on the compass rose on the 175th Fighter Squadron flight line with a ground crewman closing the canopy after calibration of directional instruments. (Courtesy 114th Fighter Wing.)

Two F-16s airborne on a training flight carry a full weapons load in a photograph taken from an adjacent 175th Fighter Squadron F-16. (Courtesy 114th Fighter Wing.)

A 175th Fighter Squadron F-16 and personnel deployed to Al Jabar Air Base, Kuwait, are pictured in April 1998. The squadron was deployed in support of Operational Southern Watch. A partially destroyed hardened concrete aircraft shelter is in the background. (Courtesy 114th Fighter Wing.)

Shown are deployed F-16s (right front to back: Richmond, Virginia; and Sioux Falls, South Dakota; and left front to back: Buckley, Colorado; and Sioux Falls, South Dakota) from Air National Guard units. A total of 11 F-16s and 185 personnel were deployed to Incirlik Air Base, Turkey, to support Operation Provide Comfort II to protect innocent people from annihilation by the Iraqi military. (Courtesy 114th Fighter Wing.)

This is an interesting photograph of a 175th Fighter Squadron F-16 taken around July–August 2008 at Camp Anaconda, later renamed Joint Base Ballard, Iraq, in support of Operation Iraqi Freedom. The murky conditions resulted from a five-day dust storm, called a haboob. (Courtesy 114th Fighter Wing.)

An F-16 from the 175th Fighter Squadron is on the flight line with a pilot in the cockpit and a crewman by the left wing prior to a training flight. (Courtesy 114th Fighter Wing.)

An F-16 is on final approach with its landing gear down and locked while heading toward Joe Foss Field in this photograph taken from an adjacent F-16. (Courtesy 114th Fighter Wing.)

An F-16 is over snow-covered South Dakota ranchland in this image captured from an adjacent F-16. (Courtesy 114th Fighter Wing.)

F-16s are parked on the 175th Fighter Squadron flight line. Fire extinguishers and plastic-covered mechanics toolboxes sit alongside. (Courtesy 114th Fighter Wing.)

During Snow Bird 1993, this 175th Fighter Squadron F-16 sits inside an aircraft shelter on Hill Air Force Base, Utah. This is a head-on photograph of the F-16 showing the air intake covered. (Courtesy 114th Fighter Wing.)

An F-16 is inside a maintenance hangar with an airman working inside the left side of the cockpit and another off the left-side nose of the aircraft. Interesting items to the left side of the photograph are tricycles and bicycles used to lessen the number of motorized vehicles around the aircraft. (Courtesy 114th Fighter Wing.)

An F-16 is inside an engine test chamber with the engine running under close examination by two engine mechanics under the right rear of the aircraft. They are wearing protective ear coverings, not seen due to the landing gear blocking the ground-level view. (Courtesy 114th Fighter Wing.)

The F-16 in the foreground is parked on the compass rose with a line of more 175th Fighter Squadron F-16s on the flight line. (Courtesy 114th Fighter Wing.)

Four F-16s from South Dakota Air National Guard fly on formation past Mount Rushmore Memorial in the southern Black Hills, with the photograph taken from an adjacent 175th Fighter Squadron F-16. (Courtesy 114th Fighter Wing.)

A General Dynamics F-16 Fighting Falcon with a pilot in the cockpit, canopy closed, prepares to taxi out of the parking slot on the flight line to the runway for takeoff to begin a training flight. (Courtesy 114th Fighter Wing.)

This is a group photograph of Air National Guard unit F-16s and personnel participating in Operation Provide Comfort, deployed to Incirlik Air Base, Turkey. (Courtesy 114th Fighter Wing.)

This is a head-on view of an F-16 at Snow Bird 1993 deployment at Hill Air Force Base. (Courtesy 114th Fighter Wing.)

An F-16 is on the 175th Fighter Squadron flight line with a pilot in the cockpit, canopy closed, and a ground crewman directs the pilot to begin taxiing onto the runway for the start of a training flight. (Courtesy 114th Fighter Wing.)

Four F-16s are in formation over the western South Dakota Black Hills in this photograph taken from an adjacent 175th Fighter Squadron F-16. (Courtesy 114th Fighter Wing.)

Three F-16s are parked on the flight line with a concrete engine blast deflector in the background to protect the hangar on the other side of the concrete barrier. (Courtesy 114th Fighter Wing.)

An F-16 is airborne with a training air-to-air missile on each wing. (Courtesy 114th Fighter Wing.)

The possible future aircraft for the South Dakota Air National Guard is the Lockheed Martin F-35A Lightning II, such as this one on the 175th Fighter Squadron flight line, assigned to the 419th Fighter Wing at Hill Air Force Base, Utah. (Courtesy 114th Fighter Wing.)

Shown is an F-16 Fighting Falcon taking off from the Sioux Falls Airport runway for a training flight to maintain pilot proficiency and obtain the required monthly flight hours. The Federal Aviation Authority (FAA) control tower is visible in the background. Control is essential since this is a busy commercial airport. (Courtesy 114th Fighter Wing.)

This is a close-up view of four 114th Fighter Wing F-16 Fighting Falcons, with Mount Rushmore Memorial in the background. These South Dakota Air National Guard fighters were documented from an adjacent F-16. (Courtesy 114th Fighter Wing.)

A former 114th Fighter Wing F-16 Fighting Falcon, a Block 30 aircraft, is on display at the wing's outdoor aircraft display area. (Courtesy 114th Fighter Wing.)

This is a photograph of the wing change during a command ceremony that welcomed the new commander for the 114th Fighter Wing on September 7, 2019. Col. Mark R. Morrell took command from Col. Nathan B. Alholinna, with the ceremony presided over by Brig. Gen. Russ A. Waltz, assistant adjutant general for Air, South Dakota National Guard. (Courtesy 114th Fighter Wing.)

This photograph shows the rollout ceremony of the Lockheed F-35A Lighting II fighter at the Lockheed production facility. A few Air National Guard units have been equipped with the F-35A, with more scheduled as production increases. The South Dakota Air National Guard is somewhere in the replacement pipeline schedule if authorization is approved by the Air Force. (Courtesy Lockheed Martin Public Affairs.)

Shown is a Lockheed F-35 Lighting II fighter, 388th Fighter Wing, Hill Air Force Base, during a training exercise approaching a refueling position on the flight line. (Courtesy 75th Air Base Wing.)

Shown is the 114th Fighter Wing patch, worn by the pilots of the South Dakota Air National Guard and assigned personnel. (Courtesy 114th Fighter Wing.)

This is a photograph of an inactivated Lockheed F-16 Fighting Falcon, Block 30, flown by the 114th Fighter Wing, now on display at the wing's airpark. (Courtesy 114th Fighter Wing.)

Nine

Support Aircraft 1946–Present

The history of the South Dakota Air National Guard's support, or utility, aircraft began when the Air Guard unit received two Douglas C-47 transports and two AT-6 pilot training aircraft in 1946. The pilots called the piston-powered aircraft "gas-burning, oil-leaking, propeller-driven utility aircraft workhorses" until the arrival of the first C-12F turboprops in 1985. The unit always had a lot of pride in displaying these aircraft's exterior, interior, and maintenance. Starting in 1946, there were many morale trips and support for the state of South Dakota. Many of the unit's personnel were flown on the C-47 to participate in deployments or to the National Guard Bureau. The unit also flew the state's governor and South Dakota National Guard adjutant generals on official trips. Aircrews supported the state's mission by flying flood control flights and dropping feed to starving cattle during heavy snows and with emergency medical flights from rural areas to hospitals. The unit's C-47, nicknamed "the Triple Deuce," became an Air Force AC-47 gunship during the Vietnam War. The Air Guard's support aircraft flew many mercy flights prior to the introduction of hospital and private helicopter air ambulances, as well as ground ambulance service in rural areas, which saved lives. Although there were several "dual qualified" pilots, only a few flew the unit's support aircraft for most of their aviation career with the South Dakota Air National Guard. Today, the 114th Fighter Wing is equipped with a modern support aircraft, the twin-turboprop, high-speed Fairchild C-26. The South Dakota Air National Guard's helicopter unit is assigned to the Rapid City Regional Airport.

A North American T-6 Texan advanced pilot trainer, used during World War II and into the postwar period by the US Air Force, is seen here. The instructor sat in the rear seat of the cockpit, with the student in the front seat. The aircraft was flown by the South Dakota Air National Guard from 1946 to 1955. (Courtesy 114th Fighter Wing.)

Pictured is a North American T-6 Texan advanced pilot trainer. The aircraft is on display at the Dyess Air Force Base Air Park. (Author's collection.)

The Douglas B-26 Invader was a World War II twin-engine bomber flown in combat during the Korean War and Vietnam War. The South Dakota Air National Guard flew the B-26 from 1947 to 1967 as a support and utility aircraft. The aircraft is on display at the South Dakota Air and Space Museum. (Author's collection.)

This is a photograph of the World War II Martin B-26 production plant at Fort Crook in Omaha, Nebraska. This was the first produced B-26 that rolled out of the Nebraska aircraft plant. (Author's collection.)

The Douglas (post–World War II manufacturer) B-26 was flown by the South Dakota Air National Guard as a modified cargo/utility and passenger transport. The aircraft is shown here on the Air Guard's flight line with a Lockheed F-94 Starfighter in the left background around 1954–1958. (Courtesy 114th Fighter Wing.)

Pictured here is a Stinson L-5 Sentinel light liaison aircraft flown by the South Dakota Air National Guard from 1947 to 1948. The aircraft is on display at the South Dakota Air and Space Museum. (Author's collection.)

The Beech C-45A, a twin-engine, medium passenger and cargo transport aircraft, was flown by the South Dakota Air National Guard from 1946 to 1967. The aircraft is on display at the South Dakota Air and Space Museum. (Author's collection.)

Seen here is a twin-engine Beech C-5A medium utility and passenger transport, flown by the South Dakota Air National Guard from 1946 to 1967. This photograph was taken during the winter, with a C-5A on the flight line and the World War II–built control tower visible to the right rear. (Courtesy 114th Fighter Wing.)

A North American B-25, used as a fast passenger and VIP twin-engine transport, is posed for a striking photograph on the flight line. The aircraft was flown by the South Dakota Air National Guard from 1954 to 1960 and used by the Air Guard unit as an emergency/rescue and medical evacuation transport for the state of South Dakota. (Courtesy 114th Fighter Wing.)

Shown is a modified B-25 used as a utility and passenger transport with the South Dakota Air National Guard. The aircraft was on display during an open house celebrating Air Force Day on September 18, 1947. To the left is an Air Guard P-51D Mustang, with other Air Force aircraft visible in the right background of the photograph. (Courtesy 114th Fighter Wing.)

Two modified B-25s are positioned on the South Dakota Air National Guard flight line. The B-25 to the left shows standard Air Force markings, and the second to the right bears no paint but shows the factory silver aluminum finish. (Courtesy 114th Fighter Wing.)

This is a close-up view of the left side of a B-25, with a pilot pointing to the "Lobo" logo below the pilot's cockpit window. (Courtesy 114th Fighter Wing.)

Shown is a Douglas C-47 Skytrain airborne over South Dakota ranchland during a blizzard dropping hay to feed cattle and supplies for isolated families. The aircraft was flown by the South Dakota Air National Guard from 1946 to 1967. (Courtesy 114th Fighter Wing.)

The Douglas C-47 Skytrain, a twin-engine cargo/utility and passenger transport, was flown by the South Dakota Air National Guard. This aircraft is on display at the South Dakota Air and Space Museum. (Author's collection.)

Two Douglas C-47s are on the South Dakota Air National Guard flight line. Both aircraft have the left passenger doors open, with the right doors closed; these were used to load oversize cargo into the aircraft. The C-47 on the right of the photograph is serial no. 0-293222, nicknamed the "Triple Deuce." (Courtesy 114th Fighter Wing.)

The Douglas C-54 Skymaster served as a long-range cargo and passenger airliner. It was considered a heavy transport during World War II and into the Cold War, as highlighted during the Berlin Airlift in 1949. The aircraft was flown by the South Dakota Air National Guard from 1967 to 1975. This aircraft is on display at the South Dakota Air and Space Museum. (Author's collection.)

From 1973 to 1975, the twin-engine Douglas T-29 was flown by the South Dakota Air National Guard as a fast transport and utility aircraft. (Courtesy 114th Fighter Wing.)

This is a photograph of the Convair C-131 Samaritan, which the South Dakota Air National Guard flew in many variants from 1975 to 1985. The Air Guard used the aircraft as a medical evacuation, VIP, and utility/passenger transport. (Courtesy 114th Fighter Wing.)

Pictured is the left-side view of a Convair C-131 with its passenger door open and fitted with internally mounted passenger steps. It was a popular transport aircraft with members of the South Dakota Air National Guard. (Courtesy 114th Fighter Wing.)

The Douglas T-29 was used as a medium cargo transport by the South Dakota Air National Guard from 1973 to 1975. (Courtesy 114th Fighter Wing.)

Shown is a Beechcraft C-12 Huron aircraft, flown by the South Dakota Air National Guard from 1993 to 1995 as a high-speed transport, VIP, and passenger aircraft. (Courtesy 114th Fighter Wing.)

The South Dakota Air National Guard was first equipped with the Fairchild C-26 in 1995. The twin-turboprop, high-speed passenger and VIP aircraft continues to fly with the 114th Fighter Wing. (Courtesy 114th Fighter Wing.)

Ten

Facilities 1946–Present

During World War II, the US Army Corps of Engineers built Sioux Falls Army Base, which included the site for the US Army Air Forces Technical Training Command Radio Operations and Mechanics School, with hundreds of temporary wood buildings while construction of a few more substantial structures, such as a control tower, operations building, and aircraft hangars, took place. Destruction of the World War II buildings began after the war. In 1966, a new barracks building was erected; it later became a small club and base exchange. From 1970 to 1977, the South Dakota Air National Guard complex consisted of 33 buildings, which included new maintenance and motor pool structures. With the arrival of the F-16C Fighting Falcon, there have been more upgrades and construction. A new munitions maintenance and storage complex was completed in 1995. Also completed were a new entrance gate house and buildings for corrosion control, weapons services, organizational maintenance, composite facility, cold storage, an engine shop, hydrazine storage, an electric shop, fuel systems, avionics, life support, petroleum oil lubricants, pilots briefing room, electronic counter measures, weapons and tactics, base supply, and vehicle maintenance. In 1993, the composite Duke Corning Building was dedicated. Since 2005, over $10 million of construction was completed: a new squadron operations complex, a security forces squadron building, communications upgrades and enhancements to base security monitoring and barrier systems, a new base civil engineering building, alert hangars, and base fire department facilities expansion. The year 2005 marked the 50th anniversary of the unit's base operations building, which was demolished and replaced by a $4.6-million building that also contains technology and security for the unit's F-16 pilots and support personnel. The South Dakota Air National Guard facility looks like a typical Air Force base without extensive barracks and accompanied housing, commissary, and large Army Air Force exchange complexes. It is located within the commercial Sioux Falls airport.

Shown is one of the patches of the 114th Fighter Wing. Various buildings at the South Dakota Air National Guard facility have an enlarged Lobo emblem on the walls. (Courtesy 114th Fighter Wing.)

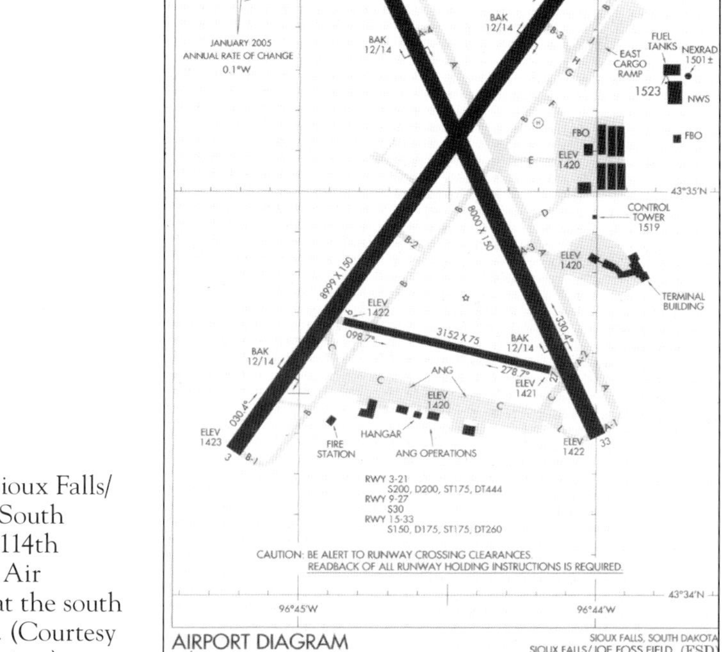

This is a Federal Aviation Administration diagram of Sioux Falls/Joe Foss Field at Sioux Falls, South Dakota. The location of the 114th Fighter Wing, South Dakota Air National Guard, facilities is at the south end (bottom of the diagram). (Courtesy Federal Aviation Administration.)

This is building No. 30, erected in 1955, which served as the base operations building until demolished in 2007. Shown in the right front of the photograph is the tail exhaust of a North American F-100D Super Sabre, flown by the South Dakota Air National Guard from 1970 to 1977. (Courtesy 114th Fighter Wing.)

This small building was used for general storage as part of the old civil engineering complex. It was demolished in 2010, when a newer, modern facility was operational. (Courtesy 114th Fighter Wing.)

Building No. 43, shown facing south, was erected in 1992 and used as a storage facility for petroleum products and other noncompressed items. (Courtesy 114th Fighter Wing.)

Building No. 33, facing north, is seen here. There are flight line fire extinguishers positioned alongside the building for use around aircraft on the flight line as required. (Courtesy 114th Fighter Wing.)

Building No. 61, facing southwest, is currently used for a base club, chaplain office, and judge advocate chaplain office. It was built in 1965. (Courtesy 114th Fighter Wing.)

Building No. 60, facing southwest, was constructed in 1959 and nicknamed the "Palace." The 114th wing commander, his support staff, and chow halls have been in this building, permanently functioning under many different sections, including a medical clinic. (Courtesy 114th Fighter Wing.)

Building No. 64, facing northeast, was erected in 1994. It now contains the medical clinic, finance office, and communications. It was previously used by wing security police. (Courtesy 114th Fighter Wing.)

This is a different view of building No. 64, taken facing southwest, with a static display of the North American T-33A transitional jet trainer, flown by the South Dakota Air National Guard from 1952 to 1972. (Courtesy 114th Fighter Wing.)

Building No. 63, facing northeast, contains a small base exchange and gymnasium for sports and physical conditioning. (Courtesy 114th Fighter Wing.)

Building No. 11, facing northeast, was constructed in 1976 with a large addition in 2001. Previously used as a motor pool, it now contains the air-ground environment (AGE) department. (Courtesy 114th Fighter Wing.)

Building No. 13, facing northeast, was erected in 1968. The large building contains the machine shop and sheet metal shop, with a smaller section to the left as offices for the maintenance group support staff. (Courtesy 114th Fighter Wing.)

Building No. 16, facing west, was constructed in 2000 for the fire department for all 114th Fighter Wing operations and facilities, as well as for emergency support if required from the commercial operations on Joe Foss Field. (Courtesy 114th Fighter Wing.)

Building No. 11, facing southwest, was used for the aerospace ground equipment shop and had previously been employed for general storage. (Courtesy 114th Fighter Wing.)

Building No. 12, facing northeast, was erected in 1976 as the engine shop. It is currently used for General Dynamics F-16 Fighting Falcon engine maintenance and repair. (Courtesy 114th Fighter Wing.)

Shown is building No. 12, facing west. This is the F-16 engine shop for maintenance on the turbojet power plants. (Courtesy 114th Fighter Wing.)

Building No. 13, facing west, was used for the machine shop and sheet metal shop. (Courtesy 114th Fighter Wing.)

Pictured is building No. 13, facing southwest. Note the parachute hanging tower in the background. (Courtesy 114th Fighter Wing.)

Building No. 30 was erected in 1962 and used to house the electronic countermeasures (ECM) department. (Courtesy 114th Fighter Wing.)

Seen here is building No. 20, facing west, fitted with two large doors for maintenance vehicle access. (Courtesy 114th Fighter Wing.)

Building No. 26 was constructed in 1992 and houses the F-16 weapons release equipment and maintenance shops for weapons release. (Courtesy 114th Fighter Wing.)

Building No. 14, the west hangar, was erected in 1979 and nicknamed the "New Hangar," housing avionics phase docks and other maintenance functions. (Courtesy 114th Fighter Wing.)

Building No. 40, erected during World War II in 1942 as part of the huge Army Air Forces wartime training construction at this location, was referred to as the "Old Hangar." The large hangar has been continuously upgraded, which consisted of new electric wiring and additions off the north side of the building. This book's photographs of F-51s inside a hangar were taken in building No. 40. (Courtesy 114th Fighter Wing.)

Building No. 36, erected in 1993, was nicknamed the "Chicken Shack" due to its similar appearance to Kentucky Fried Chicken franchise stores. It houses the crew chief offices. (Courtesy 114th Fighter Wing.)

Building No. 30, facing west, was used as the operations building and demolished in 2007. (Courtesy 114th Fighter Wing.)

Building No. 42, erected in 1997, houses 114th Fighter Wing supply operations, with storage of aircraft spare parts and general supplies to maintain flight operations. (Courtesy 114th Fighter Wing.)

Pictured here is building No. 40, facing west. The large hangar houses F-16 aircraft for inspection and repair. (Courtesy 114th Fighter Wing.)

Building No. 44, facing southeast, was used by Hazardous Management and for storage. (Courtesy 114th Fighter Wing.)

Building No. 44, facing southwest, was used for base supply operations and for general storage to maintain wing mission operations. (Courtesy 114th Fighter Wing.)

Buildings No. 46 and 47, built in 1942, were demolished in 2010. Prior to 2010, they were used by Civil Engineering. (Courtesy 114th Fighter Wing.)

Seen here is building No. 42, facing west. The building was used by wing operations to maintain supply functions, storage, and distribution. (Courtesy 114th Fighter Wing.)

This is another view of buildings No. 46 and 47, prior to demolishing in 2010, showing the numerous doors for vehicle access. (Courtesy 114th Fighter Wing.)

Building No. 55 was erected in 1995 for the petroleum, oxygen, and nitrogen (POL) complex. (Courtesy 114th Fighter Wing.)

Building No. 49 is the new civil engineering building, with a large interior for activities, administration, and shop areas. (Courtesy 114th Fighter Wing.)

Building No. 58, erected in 1990, was covered to protect the compressed gas tanks used by the POL complex. (Courtesy 114th Fighter Wing.)

Building No. 54 was constructed in 2001 to support POL operations with administration of their functions. (Courtesy 114th Fighter Wing.)

Building No. 53, erected in 2001, faces southwest and houses vehicle maintenance, with large doors to allow entrance of vehicles for oil changes, periodic maintenance, and repair work. (Courtesy 114th Fighter Wing.)

Two technicians work inside the vehicle maintenance shop on all categories of wing support vehicles. (Courtesy 114th Fighter Wing.)

Building No. 45 was constructed in 2006 for security forces to control access into the South Dakota Air National Guard base. (Courtesy 114th Fighter Wing.)